The African Clawed Frog or Clawed Toad

The Complete Owners Guide
By Hathai Ross

Including Aquatic Frog Facts, Tank, Food, Care, Breeding, Lifespan and Diseases.

Foreword

The desire to own an exotic pet may originate from many sources. Perhaps you're looking for something you don't have to walk.

Maybe you don't want to change a litter box. In many instances, people see a particular animal and are immediately smitten, or fascinated. It could be you just don't like to follow the madding crowd.

If you're thinking of getting an African Clawed Frog because you think this species will just sit in a tank, eat whatever you toss in, and not require time and attention, you're wrong.

This species is a voracious predator. They don't just eat their food, they attack it, ripping large pieces to shreds with their hind claws and using their front "hands" to shovel it all in.

That means a lot of water changes. Because the species is sensitive to water vibrations, you may not be able to successfully use a filter.

You can't let any metal come into contact with the water, and the tank has to have a lid or your very slippery pet will get out at every opportunity.

If low maintenance is your criteria, this is not the pet for you. Move on. If, however, you're interested in a species that is so well adapted to its function in the world it has remained virtually unchanged since the Cretaceous period, read on.

In the wild, African Clawed Frogs live in murky, stagnant water, hunting with ruthless efficiency drawing on finely honed survival instincts. Although they spend almost all their time underwater, when the need arises, they'll pick up and move to another pond.

If the pond dries up? They burrow into the ground and can live in a state of suspended animation for as long as 10 months. They handle wide fluctuations in pH levels, but will sicken and die in the presence of metal ions.

Since the 19th century, medical science has used the African Clawed Frog for everything from cloning to pregnancy testing. These creatures have gone up with the space shuttle and invaded Golden Gate Park in San Francisco.

They don't look that intrepid, with their chubby little bodies, and funny feeding behaviour, but there's something undeniably fascinating about the species. But as pets? Do people actually love these creatures when they are kept as pets?

Of course, they do. Consider this forum post from a woman who purchased an African Clawed Frog and was mistakenly told it could live in a very small enclosure.

Foreword

"I am a responsible pet owner and love all God's critters. Now that I have her, I want to do right by her. I will put her in a 20 [gallon] / 76 litre long tank and if she makes it, I would like to get her a buddy. But only when I know she is thriving. I need to know if I should put a a filter in the tank? What is the best thing to feed? I was sold blood worms, but she won't eat them. Need advice."

Regardless of the circumstances that have led you to become a frog owner or why you have decided to buy a frog, the purpose of this book is to give advice and to make sure that you do have an opportunity to "do right" by your new pet.

All companion animals deserve the best care they can possibly receive. The fact that you are here, reading this text, shows that you too are a responsible pet owner. With proper care, your African Clawed Frog could be with you for 20 years or more, so let's get you off to a good start!

Acknowledgments

First and foremost, I would like to dedicate this book to my lovely son Jacob who inspired me to write it.

I would also like to dedicate this book to my Mum and Dad, my Stepsons Lloyd, Tom and Jack and my Stepdaughter Ellie Mae. I really miss them and don't see them often enough.

I would like to thank my husband, Duncan Ross, for all the support he has given me. Most of the work was done in the evening and at weekends and other times which I should have been spending with my family!

Acknowledgments

Table of Contents

Table of Contents

Table of Contents

Table of Contents

Chapter 1 – Meet the African Clawed Frog

The African Clawed Frog (*Xenopus laevis*) is also known as the African Clawed Toad, and the African Claw-Toed Frog. It is an aquatic species from Africa, ranging from Nigeria and the Sudan to South Africa.

These frogs have been kept as pets, and used in laboratory research since the early 20th century. Since many have been released into the wild from both sources, there are isolated populations in North and South American and in Europe.

The species was first introduced to the United States in the 1920s when they were used to confirm pregnancy in women. If an African Clawed Frog is injected with urine from a pregnant woman, the frog will begin to lay eggs in a matter of hours.

(Better pregnancy tests were developed in the 1970s, and the use of Clawed Frogs for this purpose was discontinued.)

The African Clawed Frog is often confused with both the Congo Frog and the African Dwarf Frog, but the differences are clear once you know what to look for. African Clawed Frogs have webbing on their hind feet ONLY, and there are three short claws on each back foot.

The front feet on an African Clawed Frog have very distinct, independent digits, which the animal uses extensively to feed.

(This also one of the reasons you must never use a net with this species, as those tiny toes are all too easily amputated.)

Physical Characteristics

Male African Clawed Frogs reach an average length of 2-4 inches (5.1-10.2 cm) and weigh 2 ounces (60 grams).

The larger females are 2.5-5 inches (6.4-13 cm) and weigh 7 ounces (220 grams.)

The head and body of the African Clawed Frog is somewhat depressed and flattened, with small, round eyes sitting on top.

They have no teeth or tongue, and use their front feet to shove food into their mouths. Their snouts are curved and rather flat.

The African Clawed Frog's hind legs are long and robust. Each of the three inner toes of the webbed back feet has a tiny, black claw.

Skin and Coloration

The smooth skin excretes magainins, a chemical defense against predators, and an all-purpose protective coat for the frog. The substance contains an anti-biotic, and has anti-parasitic and antifungal properties.

Typically, the body color is dark gray shifting to a greenish brown dorsally, with a pale underside. There are, however, different varieties.

Varieties of African Clawed Frogs

Typically there are four recognized varieties of Clawed Frogs.

Albino

The albino coloration can present as a range of colors from a pale pinkish hue to actual deep red with purplish tones in the mid-range.

True albinos will be closer to a cream color, while golden albinos have more yellow in their skin. The "reticulated" albino has three pigments: red, purple, and yellow.

Pigmented

These specimens can be any color from black, to brown, tan, green, and grey with marbling or small flecks of contrasting colors.

It is not unusual for the frog's skin to appear solid in tone, but the underside is always a milky to creamy white. The eye colors in this variation include dark brown, amber, copper, and brown.

Piebald

When this unique coloration is present, portions of the frog's body will have no color, so that the overall appearance is something like a paint horse.

Piebald African Clawed Frogs are extremely rare, and when they do appear, are extremely expensive.

Leusitic

The distinguishing characteristic of this variety is the unusual blue eye color. The bodies are pale to white, or another color appearing in extreme dilution.

Leusitic African Clawed Frogs are just as rare as the Piebald and equally expensive. They should not be confused with albinos.

Habits and Habitat

African Clawed Frogs like warm, stagnant pools and quietly flowing streams. They are a relatively inactive species when they're not feeding, and have a long life in captivity, sometimes extending 20-30 years, but averaging 15 years.

These creatures are rarely found in running water, but they can tolerate wide variations in water pH or acidity. They are extremely sensitive to metal ions, however.

Great care must be taken never to expose their water to any type of metal when they are kept as pets. This includes any part of the tank itself, and anything that comes into contact with the water in the tank, or with fresh water you are about to add.

Estivation

If a Clawed Frog's pond dries up, the creature simply burrows down a foot (30.48 cm) or so in the mud and estivates until the hot, dry period is over.

Estivation is a period of prolonged torpor or dormancy that is similar to the process of hibernation in mammals.

The frog will arrange its tunnel carefully with an air hole in place and can then settle in for 10 months in an essentially catatonic state until conditions are favorable for it to re-emerge in the world.

Ability to Travel

The species can easily travel between bodies of water over short distances, but they only leave the water when they are forced to do so.

This ability to move between bodies of water means African Clawed Frogs should not be kept in outdoor ponds. They cannot be owned in many states without a permit, and are considered an invasive species.

Given the predatory nature of the species, and their willingness to eat just about anything that moves, the danger they pose to native populations is clear.

Trying to keep an African Clawed Frog outside is practically an invitation for your frog to head out on an "adventure." If you want frogs for your backyard pond, investigate another species.

African Clawed Frogs tend to adapt quickly and well to new habitats, and have even been known to survive mild freezes. In general, however, they will thrive in a climate that ranges from 60-80 F / 16-26 C.

Sexual Maturity

African Clawed Frogs are sexually mature at 10-12 months of age and will breed up to four times a year. They mate at night, most commonly in the early spring to late summer.

In order to sex frogs for breeding purposes, remember the following points:

- Males are smaller than females by about 20% of total body mass.

- Because they have no cloaca, their rump is flat, and their bodies and legs are slim.

- The forearms of male frogs sport black spots known as "nuptial pads."

- Males call out to females during mating season with a sound not unlike the chirping of a cricket.

Not only are the females larger, they are also pear-shaped with decidedly chubby legs. Other distinguishing marks include:

- The presence of a small bump between the legs that indicates the location of the cloaca, the spot from which waste is passed and eggs are deposited.

- There are no black marks on the front legs, but the palms of the "hands" can be smoky in appearance.

Females, unlike males, do not sing or call back to the males. Their sign of acceptance is a soft "rapping" sound, while they indicate rejection of a potential mate with a slow ticking.

Life as a Predator

Although a rather placid looking creature, African Clawed Frogs are carnivores and highly skilled, voracious predators. They will attack anything that moves and they will eat anything they can find.

Needless to say, this does not make them a good roommate for any other species! Don't plan on putting anything living in the tank with your frog unless you are intentionally giving your pet a snack.

Feeding Behavior

The frog uses its powerful hind legs and claws to shred food, which it then picks up and crams into its mouth using its front feet in a very "hand-like" fashion. Watching a Clawed Frog eat may not be a task for the weak of stomach, but it is fascinating.

They are, however, very messy feeders in captivity, which is part of what necessitates a great deal of housework on the part of their keepers. The water in the tank will foul quickly, so get used to the idea of a lot of water changes.

In the wild, females tend to quietly hunt in the areas above the surface of the water looking for their next meal, while males search the bottom relentlessly for food.

Sensory Lateral Line

Because the African Clawed Frog is a native of dim, murky water, one of their most useful adaption's is their sensory lateral line. This organ allows the frog to sense vibrations in the surrounding water.

While a highly efficient means of hunting in the wild, the presence of the lateral line can be a challenging aspect of keeping a Clawed Frog as a pet. Basically, the frogs can feel whatever is going on in the water around them.

Many enthusiasts refuse to use filters in the water, believing that subjecting this sensitive creature to the constant vibration of a pump is cruel, and results in severe stress.

Since a filter must run constantly in order to do its job, having one in the tank means the frogs are never free of the "noise" the filter creates in the water.

Legal Status

African Clawed Frogs are regarded an invasive pest species. Even when keeping these creatures as pets, you must consider the legal ramifications of ownership in your area.

If released, these frogs will devastate a local frog population and establish dominance very quickly. African Clawed Frogs are highly adaptable, and very good at what they do.

It is essential that if you keep a companion African Clawed Frog, and need to get rid of the animal for any reason that the frog be placed with another caregiver, not released in the wild.

Additionally, it is possible for African clawed frogs to carry a deadly fungus, *Batrachochytrium dendrobatis*, that is linked to the serious decline of more than 200 species of amphibians around the world.

The disease, which will be discussed more fully in the chapter on African Clawed Frog Health, is transmitted though spores in the water.

These spores tunnel into the affected animal's skin, causing it to thicken. Systemically, the animal's electrolytes then become imbalanced, and the brain begins to swell.

African Clawed Frogs are principally carriers of this pathogen, which is proving to be a scourge to all types of amphibians around the world.

Illegal States

It is illegal to own, transport, or sell an African Clawed Frog without a permit in the following states:

- Arizona
- California
- Kentucky
- Louisiana
- New Jersey
- North Carolina
- Oregon
- Virginia
- Hawaii
- Nevada
- Washington
- Ohio

Chapter 1 – Meet the African Clawed Frog

It is illegal to own African Clawed Frogs in much of Canada. (You should always check with the local authorities before acquiring one of these creatures as a companion.)

In the United Kingdom, there is is no requirement to have a permit to keep this species, however it is recommended that you check with your local council before you buy.

The problem of illegal release is just as serious in the UK, where a known feral colony of African Clawed Frogs was recently discovered in South Wales.

Chapter 1 – Meet the African Clawed Frog

African Clawed Frogs as Pets?

Obviously you wouldn't be reading this book if you weren't interested in having a pet frog, and I wouldn't be writing it if I couldn't attest to the rather exceptional personality of these creatures.

Although they are fully aquatic frogs, and must stay in their tank at all times, they become quite interested in the world around them.

Clawed Frogs are certainly capable of recognizing their keeper and other family members, and will often come to the top of the water for a few moments of "conversation."

Since they will eat anything that moves, there's no trick to teaching a Clawed Frog to eat out of your hand. Just wiggle something in front of his nose!

Don't worry about getting bitten. Your frog has no teeth, and at most you'll feel a little pressure if he does catch your finger in his mouth.

(If you're concerned or timid about this prospect, offer the treat at the end of a pair of forceps.)

Don't Underestimate Longevity

When I was researching material for this text, I ran across an all too typical story on an amphibian discussion forum. Most parents will have experienced some variation of this story with a pet they "inherited" when their son or daughter left home for college or to marry.

The forum poster, a father, bought an African Clawed Frog for his 10-year-old son thinking the creature would be a fun and short-lived pet. The boy did, indeed, like the frog, and the creature thrived.

In time, the son graduated high school and went to college. The frog lived on – still thriving. The son married and had a child of his own. The frog lived on – in fact, he didn't seem to be aging at all!

At the time the poster was writing in the forum, the pet was entering his 20th year, still enjoying his habitat, which they redecorated from time to time — more to address their own boredom than the frog's.

The most commonly mouthed words by visitors to the home had become, "Is that thing STILL alive?"

Don't get a Clawed Frog — or any pet — if you're not prepared to give it the time, attention, and care it deserves. That could mean a commitment that might last for years and years and years!

Understand that from the beginning. Although the father's tone was somewhat rueful about the frog's life span, it was also obvious that he was taking good care of what he once thought of as a "throw away" pet.

Chapter 1 – Meet the African Clawed Frog

There are no "throw away" pets, including African Clawed Frogs.

Fun Facts About African Clawed Frogs

- African Clawed Frogs are the only amphibian with claws, which the creature uses to shred its food. The front feet have "fingers" the frog uses to stuff its mouth.

- The species has been known to science since the 19th century. Many introduced populations started with lab animals that were released in the wild.

- In the 1920s, it was discovered that if an African Clawed Frog is injected with urine from a pregnant woman, the frog will begin to lay eggs in a matter of hours. The species was used in pregnancy testing until the 1970s.

- The African Clawed Frog was the first invertebrate to be cloned in laboratory experiments.

- When the Space Shuttle Endeavor lifted off on September 12, 1992, several African Clawed Frogs were onboard as part of an experiment in reproduction and development in zero gravity.

- The skin of an African Clawed Frog excretes powerful substances called magainins that are antibiotics with antifungal and antiparasitic properties. They protect the frogs in their murky natural habitats and also repel predators.

- In dry conditions, an African Clawed Frog can lie dormant in its burrow for almost a year.

Fun Facts About African Clawed Frogs

- African Clawed Frogs spend most of their time underwater, but they do come to the surface to breathe. They have well-developed lungs, but not much cutaneous respiration.

Chapter 2 – Buying an African Clawed Frog

Because you are contemplating buying a fully aquatic species, make the decision to purchase an African Clawed Frog BEFORE you walk into the pet store.

Buy everything your frog will need and have the environment ready for your new pet as soon as you bring it home.

What to Know Before You Buy

No pet should ever be purchased as an impulse buy, especially a species like the African Clawed Frog, which depends on good water quality to thrive and requires frequent tank maintenance.

Chapter 2 – Buying an African Clawed Frog

The first thing you should ask yourself is simply if you have room in your home for the aquarium. African Clawed Frogs need long tanks that may be harder to place in your environment.

Are you willing – and able – to provide the food an amphibious species requires? This includes live food, so the "ick" factor must be taken into account.

(If you're trying to save money, you may even consider raising your frog's food, which is extra work. Try to judge accurately how much you're willing to take on.)

African Clawed Frogs live a long time – as much as 20 years. Are you willing to commit years to caring for an animal that simply cannot be released into the wild?

Not only is wild release illegal in many states, it is also irresponsible. These vicious predators can easily overwhelm native populations, and they can spread disease.

(Yes, I keep saying that for a reason. Do NOT turn one of these frogs loose. EVER!)

As an invasive species with the capacity to overwhelm existing populations – and potentially to carry the deadly chytrid fungus – released African Clawed Frogs create a real environmental hazard.

Additionally, you must keep these creatures as solo pets. Anything else you put in the tank with these voracious carnivores will become "lunch" quickly.

Summary:

- Do I have room for the frog's tank?
- Am I willing to use live food?
- Can I deal with a pet that will live for years?
- Will I place the frog with someone else rather than release it if I can no longer keep the creature?
- Will I be happy with a frog-only tank?

Finding a Healthy Frog

Due to the increasing popularity of the African Clawed Frog as a pet, locating one is no longer that difficult. Most pet stores carry them, or can order one for you.

It is important to pick a healthy frog. You want to look for the following factors in selecting a frog.

- Make sure the specimen you select is active and exhibiting strong swimming behaviour. A frog that just sits in the tank is likely not in good shape.

- Healthy African Clawed Frogs are muscular looking creatures. The frog you pick should have strong muscle tone.

- The frog should have no sign of wounds, and there should be no fungal growth on the skin, which would look cottony or downy in appearance.

- There should be no evidence of reddening on the skin in either patches or streaks.

- There should be no missing limbs or eyes, which can be evidence of either trauma or a genetic defect.

If the frog you select has been housed with a group of other frogs, the overall group should be equally healthy in appearance and level of activity.

Summary:

- Active and swimming strongly.
- Good muscle tone.
- No wounds.
- No cottony fungal growth.
- No red patches or streaks.
- No missing limbs or eyes.
- Housed with other healthy looking frogs.

Buying Online

Please note that there are strong ethical reasons for not buying African Clawed Frogs or any pet online. While the Internet is an invaluable source to locate exotic animals, it is cruel to subject living creatures to the rigors of shipment.

Chapter 2 – Buying an African Clawed Frog

Regardless of any "guarantees" offered, deplorable shipping conditions make this practice inhumane. Please visit a pet store to buy an African Clawed Frog.

Chapter 3 – Daily Clawed Frog Care

Although African Clawed Frogs don't require a lot of highly specialized equipment, there are some essential items on their "shopping list" that will make their life more pleasant, and yours easier.

Picking an Aquarium

In selecting an aquarium for African Clawed Frogs, long tanks for lots of swimming room work best. Remember, healthy Clawed Frogs are active!

Think in terms of roughly 10 gallons / 38 liters per frog; although a 20-gallon / 78-liter tank could easily house three frogs.

Regardless of the number of frogs you keep, you may have to go to a 20 gallon / 78 liter tank to achieve the proper length required to give your Clawed Frog enough room to swim.

The dimensions on a long tank of this volume are typically 30" x 12" x 12" / 76.2 cm x 30.5 cm x 30.5 cm. You can expect to pay around $45 / £28. (Note that these tanks may have to be special ordered.)

Summary:

- Choose a long tank
- 10 gallons / 38 liters per frog

Water Depth

The water will need to be no more than 12 inches (30 cm) deep, with 6 inches (15 cm) the minimum level. Remember that your frog must be able to reach the surface to breathe.

Ideally, your frog should be able to stand on the bottom of the tank and reach "up" to the surface. African Clawed Frogs will swim a lot, and they also like to float.

Summary:

- Do not fill the tank to the top.
- Minimum level 6 inches (15 cm)
- Maximum level 12 inches (30 cm)

Use a Lid

Always use a secure lid. Even though African Clawed Frogs rarely leave the water, they certainly can jump and escape. If you have other pets, especially cats, these jailbreaks rarely turn out well.

A lid made entirely of plastic would be ideal. If this is impossible, take strict precautions not to let the lid touch the water in the tank.

Also don't allow water on the lid to drip into the tank water. Yes, your frogs really are that sensitive to metal ions! Also remember not to allow fresh water you're about to add to the tank come into contact with metal either.

Water Quality

Clawed Frogs are an unusually hardy species, but their skin is permeable, therefore water quality is of the utmost importance as it affects their skin.

Use de-chlorinated water only. These frogs are highly sensitive to toxic metal ions, which will lower their resistance to any type of infection.

This is a point that cannot be stressed strongly enough. The water in your frog's tank must NEVER come into contact with any kind of metal, including the metal in the lid.

This caution even extends to water that might drip or splash onto the cover and back into the tank. You do not want to use distilled water for the same reason.

Use water from the tap, and let it sit for at least 24 hours to outgas the chlorine. It's tempting to skip this step. Don't do it! Laziness on your part could mean fatal consequences for your frogs.

Alternatively, you can use two 1mm cubes of sodium thiosulfate per one gallon of water a day before using to clear out the chlorine.

With either approach, however, you will need to begin preparing new water for your frog tank a day in advance to achieve the proper quality and to keep your pets safe. Don't take shortcuts.

Typically with adequate water changes you won't need to test the pH levels in your tank. African Clawed Frogs can tolerate a range of 6.5 to 7.5.

If you do need to test the pH level, kits are inexpensive at around $3 / £2 each.

Summary:

- De-chlorinated water only.
- No distilled water.
- No metals coming in contact with the water at any time.
- Outgas tap water for 24 hours before using.
- pH testing not required.

Temperature Control

Don't place your frog's habitat in front of a window or any other direct light source. Remember, these frogs live at the bottom of murky ponds in the wild. They won't enjoy bright lights, and a placement near a light source makes temperature regulation harder.

Invest in a small thermometer, and keep the ambient temperature in the room in a range of 68-75 F (20-24 C). Never allow the room to rise above 90 F / 32 C, or fall below 40 F / 4 C.

Thermometers are available in a range of prices from $10-$25 / £6-£16. Some units also give readings on humidity, but this is not required for African Clawed Frogs.

If you live in a colder climate, it may be necessary to use a heater under your tank. Due to the danger of metal toxicity for African Clawed Frogs, a heating mat under the tank is your best option.

Get a unit with a reliable thermostat, which should cost between $25-$40 / £16-£25.

Any time you use a heating (or cooling) device with a tank, always use a thermometer and observe the readings throughout the day.

(Note that with African Clawed Frogs, a cooler is very rarely required.)

Summary:

- Don't place the habitat in front of a window.
- Keep the tank at 68-75 F (20-24 C)
- Don't let the room get warmer than 90 F / 32 C.
- Don't let the room get colder than 40 F / 4 C.
- An under-the-tank heating mat may be necessary in colder climates.
- Always use a thermometer to monitor tank temperature.

To Filter or Not to Filter

The topic of filtration with this species is highly controversial. African Clawed Frogs have a lateral line, which is a sensory organ used to sense vibrations in the surrounding water.

Many enthusiasts say that the use of a filter, which creates constant stimuli, is not only harmful to the frog's health, but causes severe stress over the long term.

Often you will see this scenario likened to making your frog listen to a pounding jackhammer all day. You can imagine your own reaction to that situation and empathize with the frogs.

The problem, however, is that African Clawed Frogs are messy eaters. Without filtration in their tank, the water will become fouled quickly, greatly enhancing your maintenance chores. You could be looking at changing the water every day.

It's best to look for a filter with a variable control that will allow for a slow, gentle setting. You can also divert the output of the filter against the wall of the tank or some decoration to minimize water flow and reduce stress.

Opting for gentle filtration will help to keep the tank cleaner, but watch your frog closely for any signs of stress. Decrease the flow or discontinue use of the filter if it seems to be triggering an adverse reaction in your pet.

Shop for tank filters rated specifically for use with reptiles. Many of these units are designed to accommodate water levels as low as 2 inches / 5 cm.

Remember that the minimum water level minimum for African Clawed Frogs is 6 inches/ 15 cm.

Tetra makes a line of Whisper In Tank reptile filters rated in capacity from 2 gallon (7.5 liter) to 20 gallon (76 liter). These units range in price from $7-$15 / £4-£9.

Summary:

- African Clawed Frogs have a sensory lateral line.
- They can feel vibrations in the water.
- Use a variable control filter set on low.
- Watch your pet for signs of stress.

Lighting

African Clawed Frogs do not need any special lighting, but prefer indirect light sources on a 12-hour light and dark cycle. Be sure to turn the light off at night.

An LED light could well be your best option, as they will interfere less with temperature control. These units are slightly more expensive than traditional lamps, but they use 80% less electricity and the bulbs burn for years.

Expect to spend $50-$100 / £31-£62.

Summary:

- African Clawed Frogs do not need special lighting.
- They don't like direct lights.
- They do like subdued lighting.
- Use a 12-hour light/dark cycle.
- Turn the tank lights off at night.
- LED lights are more economical and efficient, and create a quality of light the frogs should find ideal.

Substrate and Decorations

Lighting, substrate, and decorations help to create the aesthetic look of your frog tank. After all, the tank will be a part of your home. You want it to look nice, and be a stimulating and appropriate environment for your pet.

You can choose almost any kind of substrate – even just a dark cloth under a bare tank floor, which will make the frogs feel more secure, while making tank maintenance easier for you

Some frog keepers feel that this approach is, essentially, the path of least resistance on many levels. There are some specific concerns associated with using gravel with this species.

African Clawed Frogs will swallow small bits of gravel, which can become lodged in their digestive tract. Your pet should be able to pass anything under the size of a pea, but you may not want to take the risk.

Some people use aquarium sealant to permanently glue gravel to the bottom of the tank, but that arrangement will require you to vacuum out accumulated debris.

Alternately, you can opt for large river stones that create a "river bed." Bigger rocks can be moved more easily for cleaning, but accumulated feces and leftover food will still work their way underneath the layer.

Fine aquarium sand will work as a substrate, but if it gets stirred up, it contributes to water fouling and can interfere with filter function.

These frogs like hiding places. Good choices are rock formations that you create. Take a simple terra cotta flower pot, break a hole in the side, and place rocks around it to make a frog "cave."

You can include wood decorations, but make sure the item won't leach dyes or chemicals into the water. Just picking up driftwood in the wild isn't a good idea since you don't know with what it's come into contact.

Artificial plants are your best bet since the frogs will dig up any live plants.

Creating hiding spots gives your African Clawed Frogs a greater sense of security, and this allows you an opportunity to create a serviceable environment for your pet that also looks good in your home.

Depending on materials chosen, budget about $30 / £19 to decorate your frog's tank.

Summary:

- Substrate and decorations make the tank more appealing.
- Don't use gravel smaller than the size of a pea.
- Sand may foul the water and clog the filter.
- Provide hiding spaces to make your frogs feel safer.
- Don't use any decorations that will leach chemicals.
- Use artificial plants. The frogs will dig up living plants.

Diet

African Clawed Frogs aren't hard to feed. They don't care if their food is alive or dead, and they enjoy variety.

Floating reptile sticks like Reptomin will be a staple of your pet's kitchen (10.5 oz./ 298 grams, $9 / £6), along with such items as:

- bloodworms (1.68 ounces / 47.6 grams, $6 / £4)

- wax worms (300 count, $10 / £6)
- brine shrimp (freeze dried, 3 ounces / 85 grams, $12 / £8)

Earthworms can be an excellent "do-it-yourself" food source for your frogs at a very low cost. A typical price for as many as 2000 earthworms is $30 - $50 / £19.35 - £32.25.

However, you can buy a "kit" and have a secondary hobby of raising worms for just $50 - $60 / £32.25 - £38.70. And you'll always have bait on hand if you decide to go fishing!

Using feeder fish like guppies can also be a cost-effective do-it-yourself solution if you're willing to set up a separate aquarium.

Typically 250 guppies sell for around $50 / £31. Given the longevity of the African Clawed Frog, this can be a good solution, but you will be faced with tending two tanks.

If you decide to use feeder fish, prepare yourself for the fact that you will be watching one living creature consume another. This is a reality of keeping a carnivorous amphibian, but for some people the whole process gets a little too "real."

Some enthusiasts even feed their African Clawed Frogs dog and cat food. Again, these frogs are not picky about what they eat.

If you do want to buy commercial food especially formulated for African Clawed Frogs, reputable sources include:

- xenopus.com
- Three Rivers Amphibian (growafrog.com)
- Carolina Biological (carolina.com)

(See dealer sites for most recent prices and quantities.)

As long as you give your pet a balanced diet, there will be no need for calcium or vitamin supplementation.

Summary:

- African Clawed Frogs will eat live or dead food.
- Floating reptile sticks should be a staple.
- Bloodworms, wax worms, and brine shrimp are good choices.
- Earthworms and feeder fish are also good options and can be grown at home.
- There are options for commercial frog foods.
- No calcium or vitamin supplementation is required.

Frequency of Feeding

Always err on the side of underfeeding. African Clawed Frogs really only need to eat 3 or 4 times a week.

More food than that will simply go to waste and will create a lot of debris in your tank. Underfeeding is better for your frogs – and for you!

Never give your frogs more than they can eat in 10-15 minutes. If the water is not clear of food after that time, you're giving them too much.

Summary:

- Err on the side of underfeeding.
- Feed no more than 3-4 times a week.
- Feed only what can be consumed in 10-15 minutes.
- Remove uneaten food to keep the water cleaner.

Handling

African Clawed Frogs are very slippery. They can be picked up, but you must do so gently. If at all possible, however, avoid handling your pets.

Under no circumstances should you ever use a net with this species. African Clawed Frogs have tiny, fine "fingers" on their front feet that can be easily amputated in the mesh of a net.

Cleaning the Tank

In the wild, African Clawed Frogs live in stagnant water. This is not the same, however, as forcing your pet to live in an aquarium with dirty water and too much leftover food debris.

Weekly Water Changes

If you opt not to use a filter, the water in the tank will need to be changed at least once or twice a week. As soon as the water begins to appear cloudy, it's time for some "housework."

Siphon or bail out the old water, replacing it with fresh, dechlorinated tap water that has been allowed to outgas for 24 hours. (Remember, do not skip this step!)

While the water level is low in the tank, use a towel to remove any algae growth or other debris from the sides of the aquarium.

Do NOT use either a chemical algae deterrent or any type of water purifier. These substances are toxic to your frogs and can be fatal.

Also avoid any kind of soap or caustic substance, and take great care not to allow metal to come into contact with the water at any time.

There is no such thing as being too careful about water quality with African Clawed Frogs.

Remember, when you are cleaning the tank you are dealing with frogs. Be careful not to allow any escapes.

Chapter 3 – Daily Clawed Frog Care

African Clawed Frogs are pretty hard to safely catch and return to their habitat once they've gotten away from you.

Estimated Equipment Costs

20 gallon / 78-liter tank
30" x 12" x 12" / 76.2 cm x 30.5 cm x 30.5 cm
$45 / £28.

pH test kit
$3 / £2 each

thermometer
$10- $25 / £6-£16

heating mat
$25-$40 / £16-£25

Whisper In Tank reptile filter
$7-$15 / £4-£9

LED light
$50-$100 / £31-£62

substrate and decorations
budget about $30 / £19

Total: $170-$258 / £106-£161

Potential Foods

Reptomin
10.5 oz./ 298 grams, $9 / £6

Estimated Equipment Costs

bloodworms
1.68 ounces / 47.6 grams, $6 / £4

wax worms
300 count, $10 / £6

brine shrimp (freeze dried)
3 ounces / 85 grams, $12 / £8

earthworms (2000)
$30 - $50 / £19.35 - £32.25

worm farm kit
$50 - $60 / £32.25 - £38.70

feeder fish (guppies, 250)
$50 / £31

Chapter 4 – Health and Breeding

The number one way you can protect the health of your African Clawed Frog is to keep its habitat clean. Water quality is absolutely crucial to the health of this species.

In the vast majority of cases, a major water change at the first sign of illness will allow your pet's natural defenses an opportunity to facilitate healing before the frog gets worse.

The Chytrid Fungus

Although there are other health conditions that present with African Clawed Frogs, there is no more important illness associated with this species than the deadly chytrid fungus caused by *Batrachochytrium dendrobatidis*. This pathogen has been responsible for the decimation of amphibian populations around the world.

In the forests of Panama alone, chytrid wiped out 30 species. In the El Cope region of Panama in 2004, deaths in the frog and salamander populations were so extensive, the bodies of the creatures littered the forest floor.

The chytrid fungus has been responsible for massive decline in amphibian populations in Central and South America since the late 1980s and has been identified in Europe and North America.

In many cases, chytrid moves so quickly through the area -- in waves like a virus -- that scientists cannot even track its progress.

African Clawed Frogs and Chytrid

The implications of such a deadly pathogen for the local ecosystems are nothing short of catastrophic.

The major species blamed for the spread of chytrid is the African Clawed Frog due to its popularity in the pet trade, and its wide use for medical research.

What makes chytrid even more frightening is that it affects species of amphibians so genetically different some scientists liken the "comparison" as analogous to rats and whales. The implications are global in nature.

Chytrid is currently regarded as the most serious threat to vertebrate diversity in the world. It literally represents a plague in the world of amphibians.

In California, where it is illegal to own an African Clawed Frog, the species has been directly linked to the spread of the chytrid fungus, which is threatening the California Mountain Yellow Legged Frog with extinction.

Understandably, concern over chytrid makes many people reluctant to own an African Clawed Frog. This is, however, less a case of danger to the frogs themselves, and more an instance of the danger they pose to others.

The truth is that both this species and the American Bullfrog are resistant to the fungus, likely due to protective bacteria and antimicrobial peptides in their skin.

Both species are, however, carriers of chytrid. It is this fact that makes responsible ownership imperative. African Clawed Frogs must never be released in the wild under any circumstances.

Symptoms of Chytrid

In susceptible amphibians, the fungus principally affects the skin, causing it to thicken, hampering respiration. The subsequent imbalance in electrolytes ultimately leads to cardiac arrest.

In the interim, the individual will be lethargic, have no interest in food, and show marked weight loss.

Other symptoms may include:

- excessive sliming
- cloudy skin or a cloudy layer on the skin that does not shed
- impaired or partial and prolonged shedding
- excessive floating
- curling toes and nervous system damage
- a withdrawn, tucked in posture
- cringing when touched
- long periods of immobility

Some species, however, will show the exact opposite extreme of reactions, becoming increasingly agitated, and doing all they can to escape the water. This is true of African Dwarf Frogs.

Chytrid is a cool climate pathogen. It thrives at temperatures of 59-73 F / 15-23 C. In the northern hemisphere it will most likely be seen from September to May; in the southern hemisphere from April to September.

Chapter 4 – Health and Breeding

In Australia, the top end of the country is normally too hot for chytrid to survive, but there are windows of opportunity for the fungus to thrive at higher altitudes.

Death follows in a few days if left untreated. Currently, the medication showing the most promise is the drug Lamisil, commonly used to treat cases of athlete's foot in humans.

The Problem of Escape and Release

This situation with chytrid and its global implications explains in large part the need for a permit to own African Clawed Frogs in many locations, and why ownership is outlawed in others.

The danger of spreading chytrid also raises the problem of releasing these frogs in the wild when they are no longer wanted as pets or needed for medical research.

As scientists work to understand how chytrid spreads, there is growing evidence that the escape and release of both pets and lab animals accounts for the current epidemic levels of the infection around the world.

This link was first made by researchers in South Africa in 2004 and is supported by a study in 2011 conducted by the California Academy of Sciences in San Francisco.

More than 200 frogs captured in the wild between 1871-2010 were tested, many of which were preserved museum specimens.

Testing for Chytrid

There is a skin swab test available for chytrid. It is important when purchasing an African Clawed Frog to not only follow all applicable laws regarding permits, but also to discuss chytrid with the breeder.

Prices for the swab test to determine if a frog is a carrier are difficult to estimate since a kit must be purchased and the swabs sent to a lab. To learn more about this process, see:

www.amphibiaweb.org/chytrid/swab_protocol.html

Other Common Health Conditions

In truth, African Clawed Frogs are so healthy, that in most cases, they heal on their own. These versatile creatures have even been known to regenerate missing toes and fingers.

The most common conditions with which you may have to deal include:

- bloat
- Red Leg
- fungal infections
- potential wounds
- gravel ingestion

Observe your frogs on a daily basis for any of the warning signs of these conditions, and address issues before they become serious or life threatening. You are your pet's best preventive healthcare.

Bloat

Also known as dropsy, this condition causes a serious swelling in the frog's body and legs. It is often fatal unless treated immediately.

If the bloat is "hard," the frog will float to the top of the tank. The animal should immediately be removed and quarantined as it has an internal bacterial infection. Sadly, this type of bloat will likely result in death.

The second type of bloat is soft and looks as if the frog has been inflated like a balloon. This type is caused by the accumulation of body fluids due to some kind of metabolic malfunction.

The best treatment is to use the medication Maroxy in the tank water. Maroxy is formulated to address fungal and bacterial infections and sells for $7 / £3.

You can also use Maracyn II and Marycyn Plus. ($12-$15 / £8-£9)

With soft bloat, it may be necessary to release the fluid build-up, but this requires the services of an exotic pet veterinarian.

Red Leg

Red Leg is caused by a gram-negative bacterium and is the most common disease seen in African Clawed Frogs. It is carried in the bloodstream, and thus can spread widely in a short period of time.

Red Leg causes the upper thighs to become swollen and red. The disease spreads next to the abdomen, and if left untreated, the flesh begins to disintegrate and literally detach from the body. At this point, euthanasia is the only option.

The most important thing to know is that keeping a clean tank with good water conditions will prevent Red Leg altogether!

If your frog does begin to show signs of Red Leg, treat the condition immediately with antibiotics like Maracyn II and Marycyn Plus. ($12-$15 / £8-£9)

The frog should be isolated from other tank inhabitants, and all equipment must be cleaned and disinfected. Since there really is no cure for this condition, prepare yourself for the worse case outcome.

Fungal Infections

The clearest sign of fungal infections is a white thready or cottony substance that begins to grow on the African Clawed Frog. Your pet's eyes may become discoloured.

This problem is also brought on by dirty water. Clean the tank and treat your pet with Maroxy or a similar product.

Bacterial Infections

In bacterial infections, your frog will appear lethargic and will begin to refuse food. You see clumsy swimming or an inability to swim at all.

Again, this is a problem caused by dirty water or by contamination in the tank. Clean the tank, change out most of the water, and treat with Maroxy ($7 / £3) or a similar product.

(Methylene Blue is also an option, and is available for $3 / £2. Dispense according to the directions on the product.)

Injuries or Wounds

African Clawed Frogs can injure themselves in the tank, but they heal well due to the presence of natural antibiotics in their skin.

Wounds and scratches can develop just because your pet has scraped up against a decoration in the tank.

If this happens, watch your pet closely and make sure the water is clean. If the frog begins to behave lethargically or refuses food, you may need to treat the tank with additional antibiotics.

Gravel Ingestion

African Clawed Frogs will occasionally eat the gravel in their tank. It's always best to use gravel smaller than a pea so the material will pass through their digestive system.

If you do believe your pet has ingested gravel, give the frog soft food like bloodworms to create mass in the intestines. This will help the frog to pass the gravel without developing a blockage.

Working with a Veterinarian

As is the case with many exotic species, African Clawed Frog owners most generally find themselves in the position of acting as their own veterinarians.

The more knowledgeable you are, the greater the chance your pet will receive the medical care it needs.

In this regard, the Internet has proven to be an invaluable source of support. Online discussion forums provide Clawed Frog owners with a knowledgeable community where they can ask questions about potential illness and receive suggestions for treatment and symptom relief.

As distasteful as it may be to say so, most veterinarians know about frogs only because they dissected specimens while in school.

Fortunately, there are more exotic veterinarians who are beginning to work with companion amphibians like African Clawed Frogs.

Your best bet to see if there is a professional in your area is to consult the Association of Reptilian and Amphibian Veterinarians at ARAV.org (which also includes international listings), and you can also try Herp Vet Connection at www.herpvetconnection.com/uk.shtml.

A Word on Skin Shedding

It's perfectly normal for an African Clawed Frog to shed its skin. Typically they will eat the cast off skin. Do not be concerned about this behaviour. That's also normal.

As long as the frog is behaving normally and does not have red, irritated spots on the skin, everything is going according to plan.

If, however, skin irritation is present, you need to check the condition of the tank water and the temperature in the environment.

Health Considerations for Humans

The confusion between the African Dwarf Frog and the African Clawed Frog is primarily responsible for the current level of concern over contracting salmonella from keeping African Clawed Frogs as pets.

In truth, salmonella is a risk associated with virtually any kind of pet amphibian.

In March 2012, the Centres for Disease Control issued a report recommending that neither amphibians nor reptiles should be kept in homes with children less than 5 years of age, or with people who have immune deficiencies.

Again, if a frog's habitat is kept properly clean, the risk of either the frog or its keepers becoming ill is greatly diminished.

Good maintenance and high water quality cannot be stressed strongly enough.

However, there are also precautions that should be observed. ALWAYS wash your hands before and after handling your pet, feeding it, or cleaning its habitat.

Do not keep your pet in an area where food is being prepared.

What is Salmonella?

Salmonella or salmonellosis is an illness that affects the intestinal tract. Although it is similar to food poisoning, the two conditions are not the same.

Salmonella is caused by a bacterium that is in the same group of bacteria responsible for a broad spectrum of illnesses including, but not limited to:

- food poisoning
- gastroenteritis
- enteric fever
- typhoid fever

The most common salmonella symptom in humans is severe diarrhoea. Other symptoms include:

- abdominal cramps
- blood in the stool
- fever and chills
- headache
- muscle pains
- nausea and vomiting

Salmonella symptoms last for approximately one week to ten days, and typically resolve on their own. It is crucial that the affected individual drink plenty of water to remain well hydrated.

If it is judged that the bacteria have entered the bloodstream, however, a doctor will likely prescribe a course of antibiotics.

Although it is a common course of action to do so, medical professionals typically counsel against using antimotility drugs to stop the diarrhoea caused by salmonella poisoning.

Uncomfortable as it may be, your system should be allowed to fight off the pathogen and to expel the bacteria. The sooner the bacteria is out of your system, the faster you will begin to recover.

Using antimotility drugs can actually increase the length of time required to recover from salmonella poisoning.

How is Salmonella Transmitted?

Some of the most common sources of salmonella transmission in humans include:

- raw or under-cooked seafood and poultry
- raw eggs and recipes that call for them (mayonnaise)
- unwashed fruits and vegetables
- produce washed in contaminated water
- food prepared in dirty kitchens
- failure to wash hands before/after handling food
- pet reptiles and amphibians

Many reptiles and amphibians have salmonella present in their guts. They are immune to infection, but shed the bacteria in their feces.

Anything that comes into contact with their droppings, or with the skin of the animal, can also come into contact with the bacterial

Breeding and Rearing

When housing male and female African Clawed Frogs together, the animals will breed when they sense that the seasonal conditions are correct and that spring has arrived.

In some instances, altering the temperature and lighting in the room to create a "change of seasons" can encourage this behaviour, but in many cases you may not know your frogs have mated until you see eggs in the tank.

Then, you will find yourself scrambling to make all the necessary preparations. If you want to raise the babies, you'll have to get the eggs out of the tank and into their own aquarium quickly, or the adults will eat them.

Proper Tank Conditions

African Clawed Frogs will not breed if the tank or room is overly hot or cold.

If you are trying to encourage the process, change about 30% of the tank water, replacing it with cooler water to make the male frog think there's been a good spring rain.

The tank should be quiet and dark for mating to occur. It's best to do the water change in the evening, turn off the lights, and shut down the filter if you are using one.

Remember that females should not breed more often than once every three months or the stress on their bodies is too great.

Under the very best of circumstances you will have a second tank fully set up and ready to receive the eggs. Always have a plan in advance for placing the froglets with new keepers.

Remember, a female can lay hundreds of eggs. If you're not careful, you'll be overwhelmed with baby African Clawed Frogs and it is crucial that this species never be released in the wild.

Mating

A male begins the breeding process by calling out to the females while simultaneously arching his back and kicking with his legs. If the female responds positively, nature will take its course.

The male will grasp the female just above her legs. She will then rise to the surface and execute a series of summersaults, laying her eggs, which the male fertilizes outside her body.

This process of egg laying and fertilization can take as little as 30 minutes, or as long as several hours. The male remains latched to the female during this time.

Sometimes the female will rest during mating, lying on the bottom of the tank on her back, which can be quite alarming to first-time frog owners. Don't worry. Your pet is fine. This is just part of the natural process.

Rearing

When the female has laid her eggs, immediately remove them from the tank or the adults will eat them. When the eggs are safely in a new aquarium, they should hatch within 24 hours.

The hatched tadpoles will attach themselves to the side of the habitat initially. Don't feed them for 2 days or until they begin to swim freely. At birth, they are still digesting their own egg yolk.

The tadpoles are filter feeders, drawing water through special gills to extract particles of food. They will swim constantly.

Make sure you allow one pint of water (.47 liter) per tadpole to avoid overcrowding. Keep the temperature around 75 F /24 C.

Food choices include:

- Liquifyy No. 1 fry food
(1 ounce / 28 grams, $10 / £6.25)

- goldfish flakes ground fine
(2 ounces / 56 grams, $7 / £4.38)

- Spirulina powder (4 ounces / 113 grams $10 / £6.25)

Mix any of these substances with water to create a cloudy "soup" before adding to the tank. The water should be slightly cloudy. You will know all the food is gone when the water clears within a few hours.

Feed only once a day as overfeeding will reduce the amount of oxygen in the tank. To maintain good water quality, replace 60% of the volume daily with fresh water of an equal temperature.

Do not touch the delicate tadpoles or use a net with them. They should never be removed from the water. If it is necessary to move them to a different tank, pour them into a transport container filled with water.

The tadpoles will become froglets in approximately 4-6 weeks. When the front and back legs begin to grow, the babies will settle to the bottom, and they will stop feeding.

Don't be worried when the tadpoles stop eating. They are using all of their energy to reabsorb their tails, which is a major step in their growth process.

At this point, you have actual "froglets." The babies will look like what they are, miniature African Clawed Frogs.

You can begin to offer them frozen bloodworms and very small pellet foods.

Just make sure that the foods are small enough for the babies to be able to swallow the pieces.

Summary of Life Stages

Over the course of their development from egg to young adult, you will see the African Clawed Frog babies develop through the following life stages:

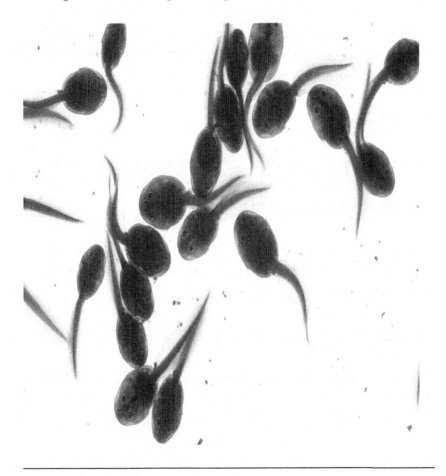

Stage One

In stage one, the young are just tiny white tadpoles that cling to the side of the tank. Dead or dying tadpoles will sink to the bottom of the tank.

Within a few days, the surviving tadpoles will begin to swim in a head down position.

Stage Two

At this point in their development, tadpoles begin to free swim and filter feed on liquid fry food or finely ground flake food for nourishment.

Stage Three

Stage three is the so-called "catfish" stage of development. The tadpoles have "whiskers" or barbs at the mouth, and leg and arm buds begin to form.

The growing tadpoles are still completely transparent, at this point. You will be able to see all of their internal organs quite clearly.

Stage Four

The tadpoles' arms and legs are now in place and the tails have begun to absorb. In this stage, the tadpoles do not eat.

At the end of three or four days, the tadpoles have become froglets. They should not be fed until their tails have completely disappeared.

Froglets

Your tadpoles now resemble tiny frogs, and can be fed pelleted foods for the next 6 months before being offered a more adult diet.

In terms of size according to rate of growth, expect the following developmental milestones over the next few months:

Froglets - (male and female)
approx. 1 inch / 2.54 cm

3 months - (by gender M/F)
2-2.25 inches / 5.08-5.72 cm

6 month - (by gender M/F)
2.5-3 inches / 6.35-7.62 cm

9 months - (by gender M/F)
3-4 inches / 7.62-10.16 cm

12 months (by gender M/F)
3-4.5+ inches / 7.62-11.43+ cm

2 years (by gender M/F)
4-5+ inches / 10.16-12.7+ cm

Note that individuals will mature at differing rates and according to the quality of their habitat.

Afterword

By now you should realize that an African Clawed Frog is certainly not -- or should not -- be thought of as a class of animal some people cruelly refer to as "throw away" pets.

With proper care, one of these interesting creatures could well be your companion for 20 years or more.

You may not think it in the beginning, but you will become quite attached to your frog over time. It's inevitable. These little fellows have definite personalities!

There are serious environmental concerns over releasing an African Clawed Frog in the wild. Hopefully, it will never even occur to you to take such a course of action.

Wild release is not the answer to becoming "tired" of the animal or being too busy to care for it.

Due to their adaptability, African Clawed Frogs will easily insinuate themselves into an area and can rather ruthlessly overrun native populations.

The creatures can also be the vector by which deadly diseases, like the chytrid fungus are introduced.

For this reason, you must have a permit to keep this species in a number of states in the United States. In regions of Canada, the frogs are outlawed completely.

Afterword

In the UK, it's always best to check with your council before you bring a frog home.

At an estimated cost of $15-$25 / £9-£16, African Clawed Frogs are inexpensive exotic pets. Set-up costs for basic equipment run $170-$258 / £106-£161.

The price of food is an ongoing cost, but can be handled, at least in part, on a "do-it-yourself" basis if you so desire.

The major hurdle many people face when considering this species as a pet is the issue of tank maintenance. Due to the African Clawed Frog's messy eating habits, you will be changing the water in the tank one or more times a week.

(If you happen to have a frog that simply cannot tolerate the vibration of a filter, water changes will need to be more frequent.)

African Clawed Frogs cannot come into contact with any metal. They must be kept in a tank with a lid. They need a 12-hour light/dark cycle, and regulated temperature.

If these factors are deal breakers for you, this is not the companion species that should be welcomed into your home.

If, however, you are willing to provide an African Clawed Frog the level of care it should receive, you will be rewarded with an unusual pet that will come to recognize you over time.

Afterword

Your frog will eat out of your hand with little prompting, and will likely come to the top of the tank in greeting as you approach.

No animal should be chosen solely on its status as "exotic," but rather for your desire to learn more about the creature, to experience its unique personality, and to fulfil your role as its caregiver.

As exotic pets go, the African Clawed Frog is one of the more accessible and manageable species over the long term. They are interesting and engaging companions, often comical in their behaviour, and certainly intelligent.

If you've decided to proceed with your decision to bring an African Clawed Frog home, be prepared for a long association, and one that will never be dull.

Just keep the lid on the tank! These clever escape artists, left to their own devices, don't always make the wisest decisions for their own good!

Relevant Websites

Fact Sheet: African Clawed Frog
Smithsonian National Zoological Park
nationalzoo.si.edu/Animals/ReptilesAmphibians/Facts/Fact
Sheets/Africanclawedfrog.cfm

Encyclopaedia of Life
Xenopus laevis, African Clawed Frog
eol.org/pages/1038993/details

African Clawed Frog Housing and Feeding
aquaticfrogs.tripod.com/id1.html

Caring for African Clawed Frogs
www.aalas.org/pdf/frogs.pdf

Xenopus Laevis Frog Colony Care
www.xlaevis.com/

Frog Forum
www.frogforum.net

African Clawed Frog - Invasive Aquatic Species
wdfw.wa.gov/ais/xenopus_laevis/

Distinguishing African Dwarf Clawed Frogs from African Clawed Frogs
www.pipidae.net/species_determining_adcfacf.php

Relevant Websites

Frequently Asked Questions

Although it's highly recommended that you read the entire text to fully understand how to house and care for your new pet, these are some of the questions most often asked about keeping this species as a companion.

What are African Clawed Frogs?

African Clawed Frogs are fully aquatic frogs indigenous to Africa, found from Nigeria and the Sudan to Southern Africa.

They have webbed hind feet with three claws per foot. They are voracious carnivores, but are often kept as pets for their longevity and good personalities.

If they're aquatic, how do they breathe?

Your frogs must be able to come to the surface to take a breath. The recommended minimum water level is 6 inches (15 cm) with 12 inches (30 cm) the maximum.

African Clawed Frogs have well-developed lungs, and breathe air just the way you do, even though they spend most of their time underwater.

I see the word Xenopus used for these frogs. What does it mean?

The scientific name for the species is Xenopus laevis. "Xenopus" means "strange foot."

Do these frogs really make good pets?

African Clawed Frogs make much better pets than you might imagine. They're too slippery to pick up and hold, but they will learn to recognize you, can easily be taught to eat out of your hand.

The frogs will often take notice of what's going on in the room and respond to it. Many owners say their pets come to the top of the tank and greet them, even if they're not being offered food at the time.

How long do African Clawed Frogs live?

In captivity, an African Clawed Frog can live 20-30 years if well cared for. That's something you need to consider, since you should never release a non-native species into the wild.

African Clawed Frogs are considered an invasive pest species and in many states you must have a permit to even own one.

Frequently Asked Questions

What are the laws regarding African Clawed Frogs?

It is illegal to own an African Clawed Frog in the following states:

- Arizona
- California
- Kentucky
- Louisiana
- New Jersey
- North Carolina
- Oregon
- Virginia
- Hawaii
- Nevada
- Washington
- Ohio

Ownership in Canada is also against the law. You don't have to have a permit to own this species in the United Kingdom, but it's best to check with your local council before buying one.

It looks like my frog is shedding. Do I need to do something for it?

Shedding of the skin is a normal process for African Clawed Frogs. Typically they will eat the cast-off skin. Don't worry about it. That's also normal.

Frequently Asked Questions

(If you see the cast-off skin in the tank for more than a few hours, remove it.)

As long as your pet is behaving normally and does not have red, irritated spots on the skin, everything is going according to plan.

If, however, skin irritation is present, you need to check the condition of the tank water and the temperature in the environment.

How can I tell a male African Clawed Frog from a female?

Until the frogs reach about 18 months of age, it's impossible really to tell the difference.

When males reach maturity they tend to have dark red or black patches on the underside of the front legs which may fade and come back from time to time.

Females are much bigger than males, which will also become evident as they the individuals get older.

Can I breed my African Clawed Frogs?

If you plan to breed your African Clawed frogs, be sure you know how you will house, care for, and perhaps place the babies in a new home.

Also, take precautions against inbreeding. You will need a larger tank, about 50 gallons, for one male and two females.

See our chapter on Health and Breeding for information on rearing the offspring.

I've heard it's bad to use a filter with African Clawed Frogs, why?

African Clawed Frogs have a sensory lateral line that helps them to feel vibrations in the water around them. This adaption is useful to them in the murky waters that are their native habitat in the wild.

In the closed environment of a tank, however, constantly vibrating water is stressful to them. Some people liken what the frogs experience under these conditions to listening to a jackhammer pounding away all the time.

Are metals really toxic to this species?

Metals are highly toxic to African Clawed Frogs. You can never let any kind of metal come into contact with their water, including anything that splashes on the tank lid and drops back in the tank. This is an absolutely essential rule to follow to keep your frogs healthy.

Can I put fish in with my African Dwarf Frogs?

The frogs will appreciate that very much, since you'll essentially be giving your pets a tasty snack. African Clawed Frogs are voracious predators and they will eat anything that moves.

Frequently Asked Questions

Appendix I – Where to Buy African Clawed Frogs

Backwater Reptiles
http://www.backwaterreptiles.com/frogs/african-clawed-frog-for-sale.html

Shipping Policy:

"We charge a flat $39.99 for overnight delivery to your doorstep, regardless of the number of reptiles, amphibians, or inverts you buy. Please read our shipping information page before ordering. Sorry, we do not ship internationally (U.S. only)."

Alpha Pro Breeders
http://www.alphaprobreeders.com/african-clawed-frog-albino/

Shipping Policy:

"Frogs, must be shipped USPS Fedex next day! We strongly recommend Fedex next day priority." No International shipping for frogs.

Aquarium Fish.Net
http://www.aquariumfish.net/catalog_pages/misc_critters/critters.htm#Frogs

Appendix I – Where to Buy African Clawed Frogs

Shipping Policy:

Ships to the 48 continental states, with $20 in extra charges to Hawaii or Alaska. "For various reasons that are beyond our control, we cannot ship outside the U.S., and we do not foresee shipping outside the U.S. in the future. We apologize for any disappointment this causes people, who live in areas that we do not ship to. In particular this has disappointed people living in Canada, but we are unable to ship to Canada."

Grow-a-Frog Kit Ordering
http://www.growafrog.com/

Shipping Policy:

All Grow-a-Frogs are guaranteed to arrive happy and healthy. In the unlikely event that a mishap occurs, you are entitled to a free replacement. All Grow-a-Frogs are completely guaranteed to undergo metamorphosis. Should you need a replacement, you are entitled to a free tadpole or froglet, whichever you prefer.

Xenopus Express
http://www.xenopusone.com/index.html

Shipping Policy:

Live arrival is guaranteed with Next Day Air delivery. Most packages arrive by 10:30 am. 2nd Day Air delivery is available when weather permits but is not guaranteed.

Appendix I – Where to Buy African Clawed Frogs

Shipments go out Monday-Thursday, though there are exceptions.

Shipping Rates (estimated)

1 to 100 small Tadpoles or 1-4 Frogs $50.00-$60.00
5-6 Female Frogs or up to 12 males $60.00-75.00
Up to 15 Females or up to 30 males $75.00-$100.00
(Prices subject to fuel surcharges)

Live arrival guarantee: with Next day delivery live arrival is absolutely guaranteed with no exceptions unless stipulated in advance. Guarantee covers replacement frogs, if available, or credit towards next order. All claims for DOA's should be made the day the box arrives.

Will ship internationally. See site for more information or:
Phone 0033 (0) 471572246
Fax 0033 (0) 471570547

Appendix I – Where to Buy African Clawed Frogs

Appendix II – African Dwarf Frogs

Because there is a much-discussed confusion between African Clawed Frogs and African Dwarf Frogs, it's beneficial to know something about each species to ensure you are buying the correct animal. There are numerous similarities.

- Both species of frog are completely aquatic.

- Like all frogs of this type, neither has a tongue, teeth, or true ears.

- Both have a lateral line for sensing vibrations in the water.

The only time Clawed and Dwarf Frogs can really be confused, however, is when they are young. African Dwarf Frogs never grow more than 2.5 inches / 6.35 cm in length.

African Clawed Frogs are literally twice as big as adults, reaching a typical maximum size of 5 inches (13 cm.)

Dwarf Frogs are brown and tan with spotted markings. They can appear to be either speckled or "peppered." The skin may be bumpy or smooth. There is no albino variation.

If a store offers you an albino African Dwarf Frog, it's really an albino African Clawed Frog.

Why the Confusion Between Species?

The confusion between the two species has to do primarily with the tiny black claws found on the back feet. It is true that the same claws are present on African Dwarf Frogs, but once the creatures are placed in aquariums, especially when gravel is used as a substrate, the black tips are worn away.

The other key difference is the manner in which the feet are webbed. African Clawed Frogs have webbed feet on their hind legs only. African Dwarf Frogs have four webbed feet.

Additionally, the eyes on the Dwarf Frogs are positioned more to the side of the head, while those on the Clawed Frogs are at the top. The Clawed Frogs have a flat snout that displays some curvature, while Dwarf Frogs have a definite "point" to their faces.

In terms of longevity, Clawed Frogs can live 20 years and more, while Dwarf Frogs have a life expectancy of 5 years with good care.

Dwarf Frog Behavior and Care

African Dwarf Frogs are active little guys. It's not in their nature to sit still, which is the least of their charming eccentricities. It's common for Dwarfs to "burble."

Burbling is normal, but odd behavior. The frogs float in one spot with their arms and legs fully extended, but they keep one foot on the "ground." At times, they will engage in the same behavior, but will float lazily on the surface.

Distinguishing Gender

Male Dwarf Frogs are smaller than the females and have skinnier bodies. Behind each armpit on a male frog there is a small white to pink bump resembling a pimple. This is the Post Axillary Subdermal Gland, which plays a role in mating, although its specific function is not clearly understood.

Males (and females) reach sexual maturity at around 9 months of age. They hum or issue a quite buzzing "song" to attract females.

Appendix II – African Dwarf Frogs

Females, beyond being physically larger than males, also have a small bump between the legs where the cloaca is located. This is where waste is excreted and from which eggs are deposited.

With Other Tankmates

Unlike African Clawed Frogs that are vicious predators, Dwarf Frogs will get along well with other creatures their own size or larger. They are social little fellows that live happily in pairs. Any combination of genders can be housed together with no aggression.

You can keep African Dwarf Frogs in a tank with peaceful, community fish, and with algae eaters and other bottom feeders. Dwarf Frogs will not, however, do well in a deep tank because they don't swim well, and they have to be able to reach the surface to breathe.

African Dwarf Frogs can be kept with bettas, but the frogs will become even more shy in the presence of these aggressive fish, and must be provided with adequate hiding places to survive.

Bettas are also known to take all the available food away from the Dwarf Frog, so make sure the little guy is getting his fair share.

If the betta begins to nip at and harass the Dwarf Frog, the frog should be removed to a different habitat for its own safety.

Appendix II – African Dwarf Frogs

The recommended tank parameters for Dwarf Frogs are:

- Tank size 10 gallons / 38 liters or more

- Minimum 1 gallon / 3.78 liters per frog

- Maximum depth of 20 inches / 50.8 cm

- Temperature range of 75-82 F / 23.8-27.7 C

- pH of 6.5-7.5

Dwarf Frogs cannot survive out of the water for more than 20 minutes. Due to their small size, if there are other pets in the house, they might not make it that long!

It is important when arranging your tank to provide plentiful hiding spaces for Dwarf Frogs. Also, use a lid to prevent escapes -- these incidents almost never end well.

You can leave the bottom of the tank bare, just putting a dark cloth under the aquarium. This certainly makes maintenance easier. Do not use large stones with dwarf frogs. They can easily become trapped under a rock and become crushed.

Sand is a good substrate choice for a tank with Dwarf Frogs because the frogs are too small to stir up the material sufficiently to clog the filter.

Use either real or fake plants. The smaller varieties of anubias plants work well because the broad leaves provide even more hiding places for the frogs.

Lighting is optional, but you will want to turn out the lights in the tank at night. Dwarf Frogs enjoy a 12-hour light/dark cycle.

Dwarf Frog Diet

Dwarf Frogs are omnivores that will do quite well on a well-balanced diet that includes sinking fish food pellets and live or frozen brine shrimp and bloodworms.

Dwarfs should be fed once a day. If you are feeding frozen foods, be sure to thaw them first. Use some sort of small plates, like the saucers that come with terra cotta pots for plants. If you have trouble placing the food, use a turkey baster to "suck" it up and then position the meal on the plate.

If you don't provide the frogs with a plate, their food can become lost in the substrate at the bottom of the tank. This is especially a problem if you're using gravel, since Dwarf Frogs are not good foragers, and won't go looking for their supper.

A good strategy when feeding Dwarf Frogs that gets around their passive feeding behavior is to feed them at the same time every day, and tap on the glass a little before you put the food in the tank. The frogs will soon come to associate the sound with their meal and will eat better.

Tank Maintenance

Good water quality is essential for this species. Check all the tank components weekly and test the water. At least once a month, change 10-25% of the water volume.

Note that water changes may need to be more frequent depending on the results of the testing.

Signs of Good Health

You will know that your Dwarf Frogs are in good shape if they are actively swimming, eating with enthusiasm, and engaging in a normal degree of hiding behavior.

They should spend their time in the bottom half of the tank, and show clear eyes and healthy skin without lesions, white cottony fungal growth, or any red streaks.

Be careful not to overcrowd the tank, as stress is a major cause of disease in this species.

Every two weeks or so Dwarf Frogs shed their skin. This is nothing to be concerned about, and, in fact, you may rarely witness the shedding since the frogs eat the old layer. If you do see the cast off skin in the tank, just remove it.

Appendix II – African Dwarf Frogs

Selected Reading

(For readers interested in reading more broadly about the use of African Clawed Frogs in scientific studies and about environmental issues associated with this species, we have provided a survey of some of the recent scholarly literature.)

Blaustein, Andrew R, and Johnson, Pieter TJ. "Explaining Frog Deformities." Scientific American 288, no. 2 (2003): 60-65.

Boorse, Graham C, Crespi, Erica J, Dautzenberg, Frank M, and Denver, Robert J. "Urocortins of the South African Clawed Frog, Xenopus Laevis: Conservation of Structure and Function in Tetrapod Evolution." Endocrinology 146, no. 11 (2005): 4851-60.

Buchholz, Daniel R, Paul, Bindu D, Fu, Liezhen, and Shi, Yun-Bo. "Molecular and Developmental Analyses of Thyroid Hormone Receptor Function in Xenopus Laevis, the African Clawed Frog." General and Comparative Endocrinology 145, no. 1 (2006): 1-19.

Chen, Tianbao, Farragher, Susan, BJOURSON, A, ORR, D, Rao, Pingfan, and Shaw, Chris. "Granular Gland Transcriptomes in Stimulated Amphibian Skin Secretions." Biochem. J 371 (2003): 125-30.

Christensen, Jennie R, Pauli, Bruce D, Richardson, John S, Bishop, Christine A, and Elliott, John. "Effects of Ph and Dilution on African Clawed Frog (xenopus Laevis) Sperm

Selected Reading

Motility." Canadian Journal of Zoology 82, no. 4 (2004): 555-63.

Fisher, Matthew C, and Garner, Trenton WJ. "The Relationship Between the Emergence of Batrachochytrium Dendrobatidis, the International Trade in Amphibians and Introduced Amphibian Species." Fungal Biology Reviews 21, no. 1 (2007): 2-9.

Gouchie, GM, Roberts, LF, and Wassersug, RJ. "The Effect of Mirrors on African Clawed Frog (xenopus Laevis) Larval Growth, Development, and Behavior." Behavioral Ecology and Sociobiology 62, no. 11 (2008): 1821-29.

Green, Sherril L, Lifland, Barry D, Bouley, Donna M, Brown, Barbara A, Wallace, RJ, and Ferrell, JE. "Disease Attributed to Mycobacterium Chelonae in South African Clawed Frogs (xenopus Laevis)." Comparative Medicine 50, no. 6 (2000): 675-79.

Guénette, Sarah A, Hélie, Pierre, Beaudry, Francis, and Vachon, Pascal. "Eugenol for Anesthesia of African Clawed Frogs (xenopus Laevis)." Veterinary Anaesthesia and Analgesia 34, no. 3 (2007): 164-70.

Gayes, Tyrone B, Case, Paola, Chui, Sarah, Chung, Duc, Haeffele, Cathryn, Haston, Kelly, Lee, Melissa, Mai, Vien Phoung, Marjuoa, Youssra, and Parker, John. "Pesticide Mixtures, Endocrine Disruption, and Amphibian Declines: Are We Underestimating the Impact?" Environmental Health Perspectives 114, no. S-1 (2006): 40.

Selected Reading

Hayes, Tyrone B, Khoury, Vicky, Narayan, Anne, Nazir, Mariam, Park, Andrew, Brown, Travis, Adame, Lillian, Chan, Elton, Buchholz, Daniel, and Stueve, Theresa. "Atrazine Induces Complete Feminization and Chemical Castration in Male African Clawed Frogs (xenopus Laevis)." Proceedings of the National Academy of Sciences 107, no. 10 (2010): 4612-17.

Hayes, Tyrone B, Stuart, A Ali, Mendoza, Magdalena, Collins, Atif, Noriega, Nigel, Vonk, Aaron, Johnston, Gwynne, Liu, Roger, and Kpodzo, Dzifa. "Characterization of Atrazine-induced Gonadal Malformations in African Clawed Frogs (xenopus Laevis) and Comparisons With Effects of an Androgen Antagonist (cyproterone Acetate) and Exogenous Estrogen (17β-estradiol): Support for the Demasculinization/feminization Hypothesis." Environmental Health Perspectives 114, no. S-1 (2006): 134.

Hu, Fang, Smith, Ernest E, and Carr, James A. "Effects of Larval Exposure to Estradiol on Spermatogenesis and in Vitro Gonadal Steroid Secretion in African Clawed Frogs, Xenopus Laevis." General and Comparative Endocrinology 155, no. 1 (2008): 190-200.

Imaoka, Tatsuhiko, Matsuda, Manabu, and Mori, Takao. "Extrapituitary Expression of the Prolactin Gene in the Goldfish, African Clawed Frog and Mouse." Zoological science 17, no. 6 (2000): 791-96.

James, Timothy Y, Litvintseva, Anastasia P, Vilgalys, Rytas, Morgan, Jess AT, Taylor, John W, Fisher, Matthew C,

Selected Reading

Berger, Lee, Weldon, Ché, du Preez, Louis, and Longcore, Joyce E. "Rapid Global Expansion of the Fungal Disease Chytridiomycosis Into Declining and Healthy Amphibian Populations." PLoS pathogens 5, no. 5 (2009): e1000458.

Kelley, Darcy B. "Vocal Communication in Frogs." Current Opinion in Neurobiology 14, no. 6 (2004): 751-57.

Kloas, Werner, Lutz, Ilka, Springer, Timothy, Krueger, Henry, Wolf, Jeff, Holden, Larry, and Hosmer, Alan. "Does Atrazine Influence Larval Development and Sexual Differentiation in Xenopus Laevis?" Toxicological Sciences 107, no. 2 (2009): 376-84.

Kobayashi, RAITA, and Hasegawa, MASAMI. "Can the African Clawed Frog Xenopus Laevis Become Established in Japan?-an Inference From Recent Distribution Records in the Kanto Plain." Bull Herpetol Soc Jpn 2005 (2005): 169-73.

Kriger, Kerry M, Hines, Harry B, Hyatt, Alex D, Boyle, Donna G, and Hero, Jean-Marc. "Techniques for Detecting Chytridiomycosis in Wild Frogs: Comparing Histology With Real-time Taqman Pcr." Diseases of Aquatic Organisms 71, no. 2 (2006): 141.

Lobos, GABRIEL, and Measey, G JOHN. "Invasive Populations of Xenopus Laevis (daudin) in Chile." Herpetological Journal 12, no. 4 (2002): 163-68.

Mazzoni, Rolando, Cunningham, Andrew A, Daszak, Peter, Apolo, Ada, Perdomo, Eugenio, and Speranza, Gustavo.

Selected Reading

"Emerging Pathogen in Wild Amphibians and Frogs (rana Catesbeiana) Farmed for International Trade." Emerging Infectious Diseases 9, no. 8 (2003): 995.

Mitchell, Sarah E, Caldwell, Colleen A, Gonzales, Gil, Gould, William R, and Arimoto, Richard. "Effects of Depleted Uranium on Survival, Growth, and Metamorphosis in the African Clawed Frog (xenopus Laevis)." Journal of Toxicology and Environmental Health, Part A 68, no. 11-12 (2005): 951-65.

Osano, Odipo, Admiraal, Wim, and Otieno, Dismas. "Developmental Disorders in Embryos of the Frog Xenopus Laevis Induced By Chloroacetanilide Herbicides and Their Degradation Products." Environmental toxicology and chemistry 21, no. 2 (2002): 375-79.

Ramsey, Jeremy P, Reinert, Laura K, Harper, Laura K, Woodhams, Douglas C, and Rollins-Smith, Louise A. "Immune Defenses Against Batrachochytrium Dendrobatidis, a Fungus Linked to Global Amphibian Declines, in the South African Clawed Frog, Xenopus Laevis." Infection and Immunity 78, no. 9 (2010): 3981-92.

Reed, Kurt D, Ruth, George R, Meyer, Jeanine A, and Shukla, Sanjay K. "Chlamydia Pneumoniae Infection in a Breeding Colony of African Clawed Frogs (xenopus Tropicalis)." Emerging Infectious Diseases 6, no. 2 (2000): 196.

Selected Reading

Schadich, Ermin. "Skin Peptide Activities Against Opportunistic Bacterial Pathogens of the African Clawed Frog (xenopus Laevis) and Three Litoria Frogs." Journal of Herpetology 43, no. 2 (2009): 173-83.

Weldon, Ché, Villiers, Atherton L De, and Preez, Louis H Du. "Quantification of the Trade in Xenopus Laevis From South Africa, With Implications for Biodiversity Conservation." African Journal of Herpetology 56, no. 1 (2007): 77-83.

Woodhams, Douglas C, Alford, Ross A, and Marantelli, Gerry. "Emerging Disease of Amphibians Cured By Elevated Body Temperature." Diseases of Aquatic Organisms 55 (2003): 65-67.

Glossary

A

albino - Characterized by the congenital absence of any type of color pigmentation in the skin or hair. Generally the eyes in an albino individual are pink or red.

algae - A nonflowering group of simple plants including seaweed. Tends to appear as a nuisance growth in any kind of aquarium environment.

amphibian - A vertebrate animal with cold blood that has lungs and is capable of living on water or land. Generally starts out life in the water and progresses to a terrestrial stage.

aquatic - Of or relating to the water, or in the case of African Clawed Frogs, living primarily in the water.

C

cloaca - A cavity at the end of the digestive tract in some vertebrates (birds, reptiles, amphibians, and fish) that serves as both an excretory outlet and a genital tract.

D

dorsal - The upper side or back of an animal or plant.

Glossary

E

estivate - Animals that, during prolonged periods of extreme heat or drought, can enter a prolonged dormant stage.

F

feeder fish - Species of fish typically raised to be fed to other fish. Examples are guppies and gold fish.

filtration - In relation to aquaculture, the mechanical or biologic removal of waste products from the water and a means of aeration.

froglet - A small frog that has just emerged from the stage of life existing as a tadpole.

L

lateral line - A visible line of sensory cells in many fish and amphibians that allows the creature to detect both pressure and vibration.

LED - The acronym for "light emitting diode." A form of lighting that is 80% more efficient than incandescent bulbs.

M

magainins - Peptides excreted by the skin of the African Clawed Frog that serves as a deterrent to predators while providing antibiotic, anti-bacterial, and anti-fungal protection to the frog.

N

nuptial pads - Dark patches that appear on the front legs of mature male African Clawed Frogs.

P

predator - An animal that derives its source of food from hunting other animals. African Clawed Frogs are carnivorous predators.

S

substrate - Any material used to form the "bed" of an aquarium environment.

T

tadpole - The larva stage of an amphibian when no legs are present and breathing is accomplished via gills.

V

ventral - Of or relating to the underside of an animal or plant.

Glossary

Index

Index

A Note Regarding Photos

All photos used in this text were legally purchased from stock photo suppliers and inserted according to the purchase rules. Stock photographers grant purchasers the right to use photos without attribution. No images in this text were copied from any illegal source or used without the permission of the photographer.

CPSIA information can be obtained
at www.ICGtesting.com
Printed in the USA
BVOW06s1825061017
496699BV00010BA/211/P

9 780992 676704